Contents

KT-119-521

Sounds around you

The world is a very noisy place full of all kinds of different **sounds**. These sounds give you important and interesting information about what is happening around you.

A noisy alarm clock wakes you up. It tells you it is time to get up.

You and your friends hear each other's voices when you chat and laugh together.

A fire engine sounds a noisy siren. It warns other drivers to let it through.

Hearing sounds can warn you of danger and help to keep you safe. When you cross the road, you listen as well as look out for traffic.

Sound waves

The sound of your friend's voice travels through the air in **sound waves**. When she shouts, the air around her **vibrates**, which means it moves very fast.

Sound waves spread out as they travel through the air. So the farther away you are from a noise, the quieter it sounds.

Sound travels through water in waves too, so you can hear sounds under water as well as in the air.

Whales call to each other underwater. Their voices send sound waves for long distances through the water.

It is silent in space because there is no air or water to carry sound waves.

We hear with our ears

You hear noises when sound waves go into your **ears**. The outside of your ear is a good shape for collecting sound waves.

Your ear can pick up quiet sounds like whispers.

Blocking your ears cuts out sounds you don't want to hear.

Cupping your hands around your ears to make them bigger helps you to hear more sounds. If you block your ears, sound waves cannot get in.

You hear a sound when sound waves make the ear drums in your ears vibrate.

Animal hearing

A fox is a hunter, so it has very good hearing to help it to find food. It has big ears to pick up even the quietest sound of small animals moving nearby.

The fox swivels its ears to hear exactly where the sound is coming from.

Hares are animals that are hunted, so they need good hearing to pick up sounds of a fox or any other enemy.

As soon as hares hear an alarming sound, they prick up their ears before running away very quickly on their long legs.

Rabbits use sound to warn each other of danger. They thump their back legs on the ground.

Loud and quiet

The loudest sound that has ever been made by people is a rocket being launched into space. It is so loud that it would damage the ears of anyone who came too close.

A loud sound makes very big vibrations in the air around it.

People working with loud machines wear ear muffs to protect their ears from being harmed by the noise.

Quiet sounds only make small vibrations in the air.

One of the quietest sounds you can hear is leaves rustling in the breeze. They make such a quiet sound that you have to listen carefully to hear it.

13

High and low

Sounds can be high or low, depending on the speed of the vibrations they make. Sounds that make very fast vibrations make a high sound.

The sound of bird song vibrates the air around it very fast. Bird song is made up of lots of high sounds.

The sound of your voice comes from a voice box in your neck. It has flaps called vocal chords that make sounds when they vibrate.

When a noise makes slower vibrations in the air you hear a low sound. The sound of a bear growling vibrates the air slowly so a growl sounds very low.

A bear has a big head and chest, which help to make his growl sound loud and low.

Speed of sound

In a thunderstorm, **lightning** flashes with an enormous crash of **thunder**. The flash and the crash happen at exactly the same time.

You see lightning before you hear the thunder, although they really happen together.

A big gap between the flash and the crash means the thunderstorm is a long way away.

Light travels so fast that you see lightning as soon as it happens. Sound travels more slowly so you hear thunder a few moments later.

Echoes

When you shout at a wall you hear an **echo**. It sounds as though your voice is shouting back at you.

The sound of your voice bounces off the wall and back towards your ears so you hear it again.

A bat uses echoes to find its food. It makes lots of very high squeaks. The bat then listens for echoes of the squeaks bouncing back off flying insects.

The echoes tell the bat exactly where to find its food in the dark.

Musical sounds

Musical instruments have parts that vibrate and make sounds when you bang, shake, twang or blow them.

Drums and tambourines have skins that vibrate when you bang them.

A big bassoon has a very long tube of air inside it. It plays very low notes.

You make the tube of air inside a recorder shorter or longer by covering and uncovering the holes with your fingers.

The tube of air inside a **wind instrument** vibrates when you blow into it. A long tube of air makes a low note when it vibrates. A shorter tube of air makes a higher note.

Strings and sound boxes

A double bass has long strings and a big wooden sound box. You pluck or scrape the strings with a bow to make them vibrate and play notes.

The vibrating strings make the wood on the front of the double bass vibrate too.

The fatter strings on a **stringed instrument** make lower sounds than the thinner strings.

An electric guitar
has to be plugged into an amplifier
for us to hear the music.

An electric guitar is powered by electricity. It doesn't have a hollow sound box. Signals are sent from the guitar strings into a box called an **amplifier**, which makes the sound louder.

Recording sound

Sounds can be recorded on to tapes and CDs. You can **record** your voice. All you need is a blank tape or CD, a recorder and a microphone.

To make a recording, turn on the recorder and speak into the microphone.

You hear the sound of a recording coming through loudspeakers or earphones.

You can feel the vibrations of the sound coming through **loudspeakers** or **earphones**.

You can send a recorded message to someone far away. They can listen to it again and again.

Sending sound

When you use the **telephone**, your voice travels for long distances along wires. A mobile phone sends your voice along invisible radio waves in the air.

You can chat on the telephone to someone on the other side of the world.

A satellite in space picks up signals from Earth and beams them back to a **satellite dish** in other parts of the world.

Your television receives the signals through a cable, an **aerial** or a satellite dish. It turns the signals back into sounds and pictures.

Sounds and pictures from a television station are turned into electric **signals**. Some signals travel along underground **cables**. Others are carried by radio waves.

MAKE A GUITAR

Make a guitar with a sound box and play it. You will need:

YOU WILL NEED:

- an empty margarine tub
- 4 rubber bands of different thicknesses
- scissors

1 Cut an oval-shaped hole in the lid. Put the lid back on the tub.

2 Stretch four rubber bands around the tub and over the hole. Put the thickest band first and the thinnest last.

3 Pluck the bands and listen to the different notes they make.

MAKE A TELEPHONE

1 Push the point of the pencil through the end of each cup to make small holes.

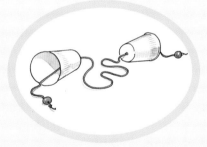

2 Thread the string through both holes. Tie the beads onto each end of the string to hold it in place.

3 Pull the string tight and have a chat with a friend on your telephone.

Words to remember

amplifier A box, which electric guitars are plugged into. The sound of the music comes out of the amplifier.

aerial A device that picks up signals travelling through the air. It sends the signals to radios and television sets.

cable A long line of metal wires covered in a thick plastic coating. Electricity and electric signals travel along cables into our homes.

earphone A device held close to or put into your ear to listen to the sound coming from a radio or CD player. The sound travels along a wire straight into your ears so no one else can hear it.

ears The part of your body that you hear sounds with. Sound waves go into your ears. Your brain tells you what you are hearing.

echo What you hear when a sound hits something solid like a wall. The sound bounces back into your ears, and you hear it again.

lightning The flash of light we see during a thunderstorm. Lightning is electricity made by tiny pieces of ice rubbing together in a storm cloud.

loudspeaker The part of a radio, television or CD player that turns electric signals into sound that we can hear.

record To copy and save sound onto a tape or CD. You make a recording with a microphone and a tape or CD recorder. You can listen to the recording whenever you want.

satellite dish A device that sends radio and television signals to a satellite in space. The satellite beams the signals back to Earth, where another satellite dish picks them up and sends them to people's houses.

signal A message that is sent from one place to another. Sounds and pictures can be sent as electric signals along wires and through space.

sound Anything we hear with our ears. Some animals, such as rabbits and foxes, can hear many more sounds than we can.

sound waves How sound travels through the air, water and even through something solid, such as the ground. We hear sounds when sound waves go into our ears.

stringed instrument An instrument, such as a guitar or violin, that makes a sound when the musician plucks the strings or scrapes them with a bow to make them vibrate.

telephone A machine used to talk to people far away. When you speak into a telephone, the sound of your voice turns into electric signals. The signals travel along wires or through the air to the person you are talking to.

thunder The crash of sound we hear during a thunderstorm. It is made by a gigantic spark called lightning that lights up the sky.

vibrate To move a tiny amount very fast to and fro. A sound is made when something moves and makes the air around it vibrate.

wind instrument An instrument such as a flute or recorder, that makes a sound when you blow into it. A tube of air inside the instrument vibrates and you hear a musical note.

Index